THE SHARK DIARIES

Other Books by Jim Toomey

Sherman's Lagoon: Ate That, What's Next?

Poodle: The Other White Meat

An Illustrated Guide to Shark Etiquette

Another Day in Paradise

Greetings from Sherman's Lagoon

Surf's Up!

Treasury

Sherman's Lagoon 1991 to 2001:
Greatest Hits and Near Misses

THE SHARK DIARIES

The Seventh Sherman's Lagoon Collection
by Jim Toomey

Andrews McMeel
Publishing

Kansas City

Sherman's Lagoon is distributed internationally by King Features Syndicate, Inc. For information, write King Features Syndicate, Inc., 888 Seventh Avenue, New York, New York 10019.

03 04 05 06 07 BBG 10 9 8 7 6 5 4 3 2 1

ISBN: 0-7407-3815-1

Library of Congress Control Number: 2003106495

Sherman's Lagoon may be viewed on the Internet at

www.shermanslagoon.com.

─── **ATTENTION: SCHOOLS AND BUSINESSES** ───

Andrews McMeel books are available at quantity discounts with bulk purchase for educational, business, or sales promotional use. For information, please write to: Special Sales Department, Andrews McMeel Publishing, 4520 Main Street, Kansas City, Missouri 64111.

To Ashley

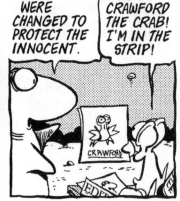

SHERMAN'S LAGOON

SHERMAN'S LAGOON

SHERMAN'S LAGOON

SHERMAN'S LAGOON

SHERMAN'S LAGOON

FILLMORE REFUSES TO SELL ONE OF HIS POEMS TO A FAMOUS ROCK STAR FOR $50,000! *IS HE NUTS?*

I KNOW WHAT I'LL DO... I'LL WRITE A POEM OF MY OWN AND SELL IT FOR BIG MONEY... I MAY HAVE STUMBLED ON THE NEXT EXPLOSIVE INDUSTRY... *POETRY!*

OKAY, I'VE SAID STUPIDER THINGS.

WHEN?

WHAT'S UP WITH ALL THOSE TENTS?

A RENAISSANCE FAIR HAS COME TO TOWN.

WHAT'S THAT?

IT'S A GROUP THAT TRAVELS AROUND RE-ENACTING LIFE IN THE 1500'S

THERE'S POETRY READING AND CHAMBER MUSIC AND TAPESTRY WEAVING...

... SOMETHING FOR EVERYONE.

MONSTER TRUCKS?

HELLO, AND WELCOME TO THE RENAISSANCE FAIR, WHERE YOU'LL EXPERIENCE WHAT LIFE WAS LIKE 500 YEARS AGO.

WE'VE TAKEN PAINS TO ENSURE THAT EVERYTHING HERE IS HISTORICALLY ACCURATE. ENJOY YOURSELVES.

THANKS.

I'M GUESSING THAT DEODORANT IS A POST-RENAISSANCE INNOVATION.

I THOUGHT THAT WAS *YOU.*

WELL, LOOK AT THE TWO SHARKS FEELING ALL SATISFIED AFTER DINING ON ANOTHER HAPLESS VICTIM.

WHO OR WHAT WAS IT THIS TIME? DO TELL.

A MEDIUM-SIZED HAIRLESS BEACH APE. FEMALE.

MEGAN PICKED HERSELF UP A REAL LOUIS VUITTON PURSE TO BOOT.

THIS WOMAN HAD GREAT TASTE.

LESS FILLING.

GREAT TASTE.

CAN YOU BELIEVE THAT PURSE OF MEGAN'S COST $1500?

IT'S A LOUIS VUITTON. VERY CHIC.

I DESIGNED A PURSE THAT'S JUST AS NICE, AND I DID IT WITH STUFF LYING AROUND THE CRAB HOLE.

CHECK THIS OUT.

IT'S A LICORICE ROPE AND A BURLAP SACK.

OOH! STYLISH AND EDIBLE.

I'VE MADE PLANS FOR US TONIGHT, MY DARLING. JUST THE TWO OF US...

MUNCH MUNCH GULP!

I WANT TO TAKE YOU OUT AND SHOW YOU OFF TO MY FRIENDS. I PICKED THE PERFECT RESTAURANT. TONIGHT'S GOING TO BE SPECIAL. COME TO MAMMA.

I WAS TALKING TO MY LOUIS VUITTON.

I HATE THAT PURSE!

SHERMAN'S LAGOON

SHERMAN'S LAGOON

OOH, SHERMAN, THIS IS SO EXCITING...

...DANIELLE SHARK IS MY FAVORITE AUTHOR!

SHE WRITES SUCH WONDERFUL, ROMANTIC STORIES.

THEY TAKE YOU TO A DIFFERENT PLACE. YOU FEEL LIKE A DIFFERENT PERSON WHEN YOU READ HER WORK.

I DON'T KNOW WHY YOU NEED THAT FANTASY ROMANCE WHEN YOU'VE GOT ME RIGHT HERE.

BURP!

COULD YOU WRITE A LITTLE SOMETHING INSIDE MY BOOK?

WHAT DID SHE MEAN WHEN SHE SAID "HUSBANDS LIKE ME KEEP HER IN BUSINESS"?

LOOK. SHE FEELS MY PAIN.

BOOKS

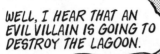

26

I HEAR YOU'RE PREPARING ALL OF OUR OBITUARIES JUST IN CASE WE SHOULD MEET AN UNTIMELY END.

YEP.

WELL, I TOOK THE LIBERTY OF HELPING YOU OUT WITH MINE.

THANKS.

LET'S SEE... "MEGAN - DEVOTED WIFE, VALUED MEMBER OF THE COMMUNITY, BLAH BLAH..

"...BEST FRIEND TO MARTHA STEWART"?

IT WOULD'VE HAPPENED EVENTUALLY!

HEY, ISN'T THAT THE EVIL DR. BRONZETOE'S YACHT?

YEP. AND HE'S LEAVING THE LAGOON.

WE EXCHANGED E-MAILS. HE'S DECIDED NOT TO DESTROY THE LAGOON AFTERALL.

HE SAYS THERE'S NO GLAMOR IN BEING AN INTERNATIONAL VILLAIN ANYMORE.

HE'S GOING TO BE AN EVIL-DOER ANALYST FOR CNN.

KEEPS HIM OFF THE STREETS.

HEADING OFF TO ASCENSION ISLAND AGAIN, FILLMORE?

YEP. IT'S TIME FOR MY ANNUAL TREK TO FIND TRUE LOVE.

I REALLY THINK THIS MATING SEASON I'M GOING TO DO IT. I'M FEELING GOOD ABOUT THIS ONE.

SO, WHAT'S THE BETTING LINE?

5 TO 1 YOU STRIKE OUT AGAIN.

HEY, THIS YEAR, EVEN THE BOOKIES ARE OPTIMISTIC.

SHERMAN'S LAGOON

FILLMORE, YOU'RE BACK FROM ASCENSION ISLAND! HOW WAS THE SEA TURTLE MATING SEASON THIS YEAR?

IT WAS FINE.

DIDN'T FIND THAT SPECIAL SHE-TURTLE?

IS THAT REALLY SUCH A BIG DEAL, SHERMAN?

ISN'T IT FAR MORE IMPORTANT TO BE HAPPY WITH ONESELF? WHY MUST SOCIETY DEFINE US BY OUR ABILITY TO HAVE PROGENY?

STRUCK OUT AGAIN, HUH?

NEVER EVEN GOT TO THE PLATE.

WHERE ARE WE GOING AGAIN, ERNEST?

THE GANGES RIVER.

DIDN'T WE ALREADY GO THERE?

NO. WE'VE GONE TO THE NILE AND THE AMAZON...

...BUT NEVER THE GANGES.

ARE YOU SURE ABOUT THAT?

DO YOU EVEN READ THIS STRIP?

I'M MORE OF A "GARFIELD" GUY.

SO THIS IS THE GANGES RIVER.

IT'S ONE OF THE MOST SACRED SITES IN THE HINDU RELIGION.

MEGAN'S READING A BOOK ON HINDUISM.

REALLY?

YEAH. A THICK ONE. IT'S ALL ABOUT FINDING INNER PEACE THROUGH REFLECTION AND MEDITATION. SHE CAN'T PUT IT DOWN.

SHE SMACKS ME WITH IT WHENEVER I INTERUPT HER.

SO, SHE'S GETTING THE MESSAGE.

ERNEST, I THINK I'D LIKE TO BECOME A HINDU. I'M TRULY INSPIRED TO MAKE A RADICAL CHANGE IN MY LIFE.

YOU'RE JUST SAYING THAT BECAUSE WE'RE IN THE GANGES RIVER.

NO. I THINK THE MEDITATION COULD REALLY HELP ME.

YEAH?

IT REQUIRES GREAT PATIENCE AND FOCUS.

YOU COULD PROBABLY USE SOME HELP IN THE FOCUS DEPARTMENT.

HAVE YOU NOTICED THERE ARE NO BURGER KINGS IN INDIA?

WHAT'S A DOLPHIN DOING IN A RIVER?

I'M A RARE, GANGES RIVER DOLPHIN. THERE ARE ONLY 100 OF US LEFT.

I'M SO ENDANGERED, YOU'RE NOT EVEN SUPPOSED TO LOOK AT ME!

I'M SO ENDANGERED, I CAN JAB YOU WITH A STICK AND YOU CAN'T DO ANYTHING ABOUT IT!

OW!

THEY'LL GET BY WITH 99... (BURP).

I SURE HOPE HE WASN'T THEIR P.R. GUY.

ARE YOU A REAL SWAMI? CAN YOU TEACH ME HOW TO MEDITATE?

I WILL TRY.

FIRST, WE MUST FIND YOU A MANTRA.

WHAT'S THAT?

IT'S A WORD OR PHRASE YOU REPEAT TO YOURSELF. IT'S SUPPOSED TO BRING YOU INNER PEACE.

UH... OKAY. I'VE GOT ONE.

FEEL LIKE CHICKEN TONIGHT. CHICKEN TONIGHT. CHICKEN TONIGHT.

LET US FIND YOU A VEGETARIAN MANTRA.

THE KEY TO MEDITATION, SHERMAN, IS TO COMPLETELY CLEAR THE MIND.

THERE IS A NATURAL BREAK BETWEEN YOUR THOUGHTS. YOU MUST EXPAND THIS MOMENT INTO A LONGER PERIOD OF TIME.

LOOK INSIDE YOUR MIND, SHERMAN. FIND THE GAP BETWEEN YOUR THOUGHTS. THAT'S WHEN MEDITATION BEGINS.

THAT WOULD BE STARTING LAST MONDAY.

I'M A NATURAL AT THIS.

SHERMAN, SOME BASIC POSITIONS WILL HELP YOUR BREATHING AND MEDITATION.

GREAT.

FIRST, CROSS YOURSELF IN FRONT, LIKE THIS.

THEN, SLOWLY RAISE THE LOWER HALF UP AND OVER, LIKE THIS.

OKAY, THAT'S ENOUGH FOR TODAY.

UNTIE ME!

ERNEST, I'VE HAD ENOUGH OF INDIA AND THE GANGES RIVER AND LEARNING HOW TO MEDITATE. LET'S GO HOME.

WHAT'S THE HURRY?

APPARENTLY, MOST OF THE LOCALS ARE VEGETARIAN.

SO?

I ATE MEAT AND THESE FOLKS ARE PRETTY UPSET ABOUT IT.

BUT SHARKS DO THOSE THINGS. I WOULDN'T SWEAT IT.

IT WAS MY MEDITATION INSTRUCTOR.

I'LL PACK THE BAGS.

SHERMAN'S LAGOON

THIS IS THERESA SCOOP SPEAKING LIVE TO CHIEF PARKS.

CHIEF, WHAT CAN YOU TELL US ABOUT THIS RASH OF HERMIT CRAB ATTACKS LATELY?

THERE HAVE BEEN A FEW ISOLATED INCIDENTS, THAT'S ALL.

WE WANT ALL THE TOURISTS TO KNOW IT'S PERFECTLY SAFE TO COME TO THE BEACH.

TO PROVE MY POINT, I'M STANDING IN THE WATER BAREFOOT RIGHT NOW. IT'S FINE.

OW!!

THAT CAN'T BE GOOD FOR TOURISM.

LOOKS LIKE IT'S LEFTOVERS FOR ME TOMORROW.

SHERMAN'S LAGOON

WOW, HAWTHORNE IS REALLY LAYING IT ON THICK WITH HIS $5 LAGOON HISTORY TOUR.

THIS ROCK, LADIES AND GENTLEMEN, IS OVER 100 MILLION YEARS OLD...

IT'S JUST A ROCK, BUT TECHNICALLY HE'S RIGHT. I WOULDN'T CALL IT UNETHICAL.

PREHISTORIC ROCKS WILL BE FOR SALE IN OUR GIFTSHOP AFTER THE TOUR.

NOW HE'S CROSSING THE LINE.

THIS, LADIES AND GENTLEMEN, IS THE HIGHLIGHT OF MY $5 LAGOON HISTORY TOUR...

I PRESENT TO YOU, FAMOUS FROM NAUTICAL FOLKLORE, THE ONE-AND-ONLY DAVY JONES' LOCKER.

THIS ISN'T DAVY JONES' LOCKER. YOU'RE MAKING THIS UP!

THIS TOUR IS A CROCK!

LET'S GO.

HEY, WAIT A MINUTE! THESE ARE REALLY DAVY JONES' AIR JORDANS! HEY! COME BACK!

YOU'RE TAKING DOWN YOUR SHINGLE? HOW COME?

THE NATIONAL ASSOCIATION OF TOUR GUIDES SHUT ME DOWN BECAUSE I WAS FALSIFYING MY HISTORY.

GUID TOUR $5

NO!

WHAT'S WRONG WITH A LITTLE FIB NOW AND THEN?

SHOOT, IF I WANT TO FABRICATE A FANTASY WORLD COMPLETELY VOID OF ANYTHING RESEMBLING REALITY, IT'S MY RIGHT!

DARN TOOTIN'. IT'S A FREE COUNTRY.

THAT REMINDS ME. I HAVE TO DO MY TAX RETURN.

SHERMAN'S LAGOON

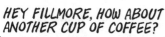

43

SHERMAN'S LAGOON

SHERMAN'S LAGOON

HMMM. THIS IS INTERESTING. IT SAYS HERE THAT ALL THE PLANETS WILL BE IN EXACT ALIGNMENT THIS WEEK.

SO?

APPARENTLY, THEIR COLLECTIVE GRAVITATIONAL PULL WILL HAVE BIZARRE RESULTS HERE ON PLANET EARTH.

LIKE WHAT?

GRAVITY, THAT OLD STAND-BY, WILL BE WEAKER. OBJECTS WILL SEEM LIGHTER. TIDES WILL BE MORE RADICAL.

MY SOUFFLÉ IS WORKING. WHAT'S GOING ON?

PLANETARY ALIGNMENTS.

THIS RARE PLANETARY ALIGNMENT HAS ALREADY AFFECTED THE TIDE.

YEP.

WE'VE NEVER BEEN THIS FAR UP THE BEACH.

THAT'S FOR SURE.

I WONDER HOW QUICKLY THE TIDE CAME UP.

HERE'S A CLUE. PRETTY QUICKLY.

SHOULD ALWAYS HAVE A SPOTTER.

FILLMORE, THIS ALIGNMENT OF THE PLANETS HAS MADE THE TIDE SUPER HIGH.

YES, I'M AWARE OF THAT.

YOU CAN EVEN SWIM RIGHT INTO SOME OF THE BEACHFRONT STORES.

NOT THE SHOPPING TYPE.

THE BARNES & NOBLE IS RIPE FOR LOOTING.

A QUICK SPIN THROUGH THE POETRY SECTION COULDN'T HURT.

THE TIDE HAS GONE BACK DOWN. NO LONGER CAN WE SWIM AROUND UP WHERE THE HUMANS LIVE.

THE WORLD THAT FOR A BRIEF SHINING MOMENT OPENED ITS SECRETS IS ONCE AGAIN OUT OF REACH.

OH, HOW I'M GOING TO MISS IT! ...WHY COULDN'T I HAVE JUST A LITTLE MORE TIME? ...SO MANY THINGS TO DISCOVER.

DID YOU SEE THE MEAT SECTION AT SAFEWAY?

DIDN'T MAKE IT THERE.

SHERMAN, I'M THINKING ME, YOU, AND ERNEST SHOULD BE A TEAM IN THE IRONFISH CHALLENGE, THAT GRUELING SPORTS-ENDURANCE RACE YOU SEE ON FISH-TV.

AND, WHY WOULD WE DO THAT?

ARE YOU KIDDING?

THINK OF THE BONDING EXPERIENCE FOR US. IT WOULD MAKE OUR FRIENDSHIPS THAT MUCH STRONGER.

SERIOUSLY. WHY?

A BIG FAT FIRST PRIZE CHECK.

PHEW! I HAD NO IDEA THE IRONFISH CHALLENGE WOULD TAKE SO MUCH OUT OF ME.

MORE GATORADE.

HOW MUCH LONGER IS THIS THING? I'M EXHAUSTED.

ALL YOU'VE DONE IS SIGN THE WAIVER.

THREE COPIES!

I JUST GOT A CALL FROM THE C.E.O. OF BIGNEWS, INC. THEY WANT TO ACQUIRE MY NEWSPAPER. THINK OF ALL THE MONEY I'D MAKE.

YOU CAN'T SELL THE LAGOON TRIBUNE. IT'S LIKE A MEMBER OF THE FAMILY.

INDEPENDENT NEWSPAPERS ARE AN IMPORTANT VOICE IN OUR SOCIETY.

THINK OF ALL THE MONEY I'D MAKE.

I'M WITH YOU, BROTHER.

HAWTHORNE, YOUR NEWSPAPER IS AWFUL SINCE BIGNEWS INCORPORATED BOUGHT IT.

HOW SO?

THERE'RE HARDLY ANY ARTICLES. IT'S ALL CHARTS AND GRAPHS.

AND, FRANKLY, I CAN'T FIGURE OUT WHAT ANY OF THEM MEAN! LIKE THIS ONE.

WHAT EXACTLY DOES THAT REPRESENT?

THE PERCENTAGE OF READERS WHO CAN'T FOLLOW CHARTS AND GRAPHS.

HAWTHORNE, I CAN'T FIND THE COMICS IN YOUR NEWFANGLED NEWSPAPER.

THERE AREN'T ANY.

WHAT? NO COMICS! WELL, THAT'S LIKE A DAY WITHOUT SUNSHINE.

COMICS ARE THE GREATEST FORM OF ENTERTAINMENT AND EXPRESSION THIS WORLD HAS.

LAYING IT ON A LITTLE THICK, AREN'T YOU?

THIS IS JUST A STEPPING STONE. I WANT TO GET INTO FILM.

SHERMAN'S LAGOON

THIS NEW LAGOON TRIBUNE IS FULL OF SENSATIONALISM.

HUH?

STORIES BLOWN OUT OF PROPORTION, OR JUST PLAIN FABRICATED TO GRAB YOUR ATTENTION.

REALLY?

WHAT'S THAT ARTICLE YOU'RE READING NOW?

MIMES: THE SILENT KILLER.

HOW ABOUT YOU?

JAY LENO'S CHIN: WHAT THE MILITARY DOESN'T WANT YOU TO KNOW.

HAWTHORNE, WHAT'S WITH THE GUEST COLUMNISTS IN THE NEW PAPER?

BEING A CELEBRITY DOESN'T MAKE THEM A PUBLIC POLICY EXPERT.

EXPERTS ARE A BORE. WE NEED DIVERSITY!

YOU MEAN, LIKE TODAY'S OFFERING?

"BRITNEY'S PLAN FOR WORLD PEACE"?

AND HOT DANCE MOVES.

AND ANOTHER THING ABOUT YOUR NEWSPAPER'S NEW FORMAT...

HERE WE GO.

WHAT'S WITH THE FRIGHTENING HEADLINES YOU ALWAYS RUN?

YOU SHOULDN'T HAVE TO SCARE READERS TO SELL PAPERS.

AUGH!

I NEED A MAMMOGRAM!

YOU MAY HAVE A POINT.

SHERMAN'S LAGOON

GET YOUR LAGOON TRIBUNES. HOT OFF THE LASERPRINTERS.

I'LL PASS.

ME TOO.

IT'S OKAY. I GOT OUT OF MY CONTRACT WITH BIGNEWS, INC.

IT'S BACK TO THE WAY IT WAS. NO CHARTS, NO GRAPHS, NO SENSATIONALISM. JUST LOCAL COVERAGE.

"BOTTOM DWELLER WINS BELCHING CONTEST."

DOES IT MENTION I FILED A PROTEST?

WELL, THAT'S IT. I'M THROUGH WITH BOOKS.

WHADDAYA MEAN? YOU LOVE TO READ.

I MEAN I'VE NOW OFFICIALLY READ EVERY BOOK IN EXISTENCE.

SO NOW WHAT?

I GUESS I'LL JUST SIT HERE LIKE YOU AND DO NOTHING.

GO EASY AT FIRST.

FILLMORE, I'VE SOLVED YOUR PROBLEM. YOU CLAIM YOU'VE READ EVERY BOOK IN EXISTENCE, RIGHT?

RIGHT.

WELL, IF YOU COMBINE TWO BOOKS INTO ONE, IT'S LIKE A WHOLE NEW BOOK THAT YOU HAVEN'T READ.

HUH?

YOU TAKE ONE PAGE FROM ONE STORY, THEN THE NEXT PAGE FROM ANOTHER.

HERE'S MY FIRST EFFORT.

"MOBY DICK AND JANE."

SHERMAN'S LAGOON

SHERMAN'S LAGOON

Hermit crab: HERE COMES MEGAN, FAT BOY. BETTER HIDE.

Shark: NOPE. NOT ME. I'M JUST GOING TO SIT HERE AND RELAX.

TUM TA TUM

Hermit crab: I DON'T BELIEVE IT. SHE WENT RIGHT BY YOU AND SHE DIDN'T TELL YOU TO DO SOMETHING.

Shark: NOPE.

Shark: THAT'S 'CUZ I DID EVERYTHING.

Hermit crab: HUH?

Shark: I'VE COMPLETED ALL THE PROJECTS. I'VE DONE ALL THE CHORES. THERE'S NOTHING LEFT FOR HER TO TELL ME TO DO, AND IT'S DRIVING HER CRAZY.

Shark: BOY, IT'S HOT. WHO WOULD LIKE A GLASS OF LEMONADE?

Shark: LEMONADE SOUNDS GOOD.

Megan: WELL, FIX IT YOURSELF.

SHERMAN'S LAGOON

SHERMAN'S LAGOON

ARE YOU READY FOR DINNER WITH THE MARLINS?

YEP.

NOW REMEMBER, JERRY'S HAD A STRING OF BAD LUCK LATELY.

UH-HUH.

DON'T SAY OR DO ANYTHING TO DRAW ATTENTION TO IT.

GOT IT.

TINA, YOU LOOK LOVELY.

C'MON IN, GUYS. DINNER'S READY.

SAY, JERRY, CAN YOU PASS ME THE HARPOON IN THE HEAD?

UH... I MEAN, THE HOOK IN YOUR MOUTH?

I MEAN, THE ROLLS.

THAT WAS FUN.

EVERY WEEK WE HAVE TO GET NEW FRIENDS!

67

SHERMAN'S LAGOON

WATCHING MARTHA STEWART?

YEP.

YA KNOW, I'D LIKE TO DO SOMETHING LIKE WHAT SHE'S DOING.

PUMMEL A CUE CARD BOY?

HAVE A COOKING SHOW.

SHERMAN, I'VE BEEN TALKING TO THE CABLE ACCESS CREW. I THINK I CAN DO IT!

DO WHAT?

FOLLOW MY DREAM AND HAVE MY OWN T.V. SHOW.

OH, RIGHT.

COMPLETE WITH JELLO WRESTLING FEMALE SHARK BODY BUILDERS.

THAT'S **YOUR** DREAM SHOW.

WHY DIDN'T YOU SMACK ME THAT TIME?

TOO BUSY. DO IT YOURSELF, PLEASE.

SO, ARE YOU GOING TO BE CAMERA OPERATOR FOR MY COOKING SHOW?

WHY NOT.

SO NOW I JUST NEED A PRODUCER.

SOMEONE WHO CAN PUT PERSONAL FEELINGS ASIDE AND MAKE THE TOUGH DECISIONS.

LOOK, MOM, IF YOU NEED AN OPERATION, I CAN LEND YOU THE CASH, BUT IT WON'T BE CHEAP.

SCORE.

SHERMAN'S LAGOON

78

Panel 1: SO HAWTHORNE WENT WITH MEGAN FOR THE TIME-SHARE WEEKEND GETAWAY PACKAGE?

YEP. I WASN'T UP FOR IT.

Panel 2: SHERMAN, DON'T YOU THINK THAT'S ODD? THEY'VE NEVER BEEN THAT CLOSE.

TRUE.

Panel 3: I MEAN, WHAT WOULD THEY POSSIBLY HAVE TO TALK ABOUT?

I'M SURE THEY'LL FIND SOMETHING IN COMMON.

Panel 4: SHERMAN'S SO DUMB, HE MISSPELLS Z'S WHEN HE SNORES.

I ONCE SOLD HIM HIS OWN SANDWICH.

Panel 5: IT'S VERY NICE OF YOU TO COME TO OUR ROOM TO PRESENT YOUR SALES PITCH.

HERE AT YURTLE BEACH TIME SHARES, WE CATER TO YOU.

Panel 6: WE INVITED YOU TO OUR RESORT TO RELAX, HAVE FUN, AND TO CONSIDER PURCHASING A TIME SHARE.

Panel 7: AND IT'S ALL FOR FREE, JUST FOR LISTENING.

YAWN

Panel 8: WELL, WE'VE HEARD ENOUGH FOR TONIGHT. WE SHOULD BE GETTING TO BED.

FINE. I'LL SLEEP IN THE MIDDLE.

Panel 9: MEGAN, YOU'RE BACK. HOW WAS THE FREE VACATION?

I BOUGHT A TIME-SHARE CONDO FOR US, SHERMAN.

Panel 10: "THE MINIMALIST"?

IT'S THE CHEAPEST PACKAGE THEY OFFERED.

Panel 11: FOR JUST $100, WE'RE PART OF THE TIME-SHARE COMMUNITY.

HOW MUCH TIME PER YEAR DO WE GET ON THIS THING?

Panel 12: TWO HOURS.

ACTUALLY ONE. OUR SLOT'S RIGHT WHEN YOU MOVE THE CLOCKS AHEAD.

SHERMAN'S LAGOON

Panel 1: SO, WHAT BRINGS YOU TO OUR TROPICAL LAGOON?

NEW YAWK'S GOTTEN TOO NICE.

Panel 2: EVERYONE'S SWEET AND POLITE THESE DAYS. IT'S TOO CIVILIZED.

WELL, YOU'VE COME TO THE RIGHT PLACE.

Panel 3: BECAUSE AROUND HERE IT'S A RUTHLESS, DOG-EAT-DOG JUNGLE. IT'S KILL OR BE KILLED, PAL.

Panel 4: FRESH QUICHE WELCOME WAGON.

I'M TREMBLIN'.

Panel 5: FILLMORE, THIS IS VINNY. HE'S VISITING THE LAGOON FROM NEW YORK.

Panel 6: SALUTATIONS, MY PELAGIC REPTILIAN COMRADE. WELCOME TO OUR SUB-TROPICAL ECOSYSTEM.

Panel 7: (no dialogue)

Panel 8: HE SAID "WAZ UP?"

HOW YOU DOIN?

Panel 9: THAT'S VINNY. HE'S VACATIONING FROM NEW YORK. THE CITY WAS GETTING TOO NICE FOR HIM.

Panel 10: VINNY, THIS IS MEGAN, MY WIFE.

HEY, ONE CARNIVORE TO ANOTHER, YOU'RE PRETTY HOT.

Panel 11: LISTEN TO ME, YOU WALKING HANDBAG! YOU WATCH YOUR MOUTH!

Panel 12: THAT'S ALL I'M ASKING FOR— A LITTLE ATTITUDE.

HE LIKED THAT?

SHERMAN'S LAGOON

HAWTHORNE, WE CAN'T DO THIS BUSINESS TOGETHER. IT'S NOT WORTH RISKING OUR FRIENDSHIP.

BUT, WE NEVER REALLY _HAD_ A FRIENDSHIP.

RIGHT...

THEN IT'S NOT WORTH RISKING ME SQUASHING YOU LIKE A LITTLE STINK BUG.

POINT WELL MADE.

YOU'RE READING? THAT'S NOT LIKE YOU.

IT'S A BROCHURE FOR A SUMMER CAMP. ERNEST IS GOING TOMORROW.

"MOLDING YOUNG MINDS INTO RESPONSIBLE, RESPECTFUL CITIZENS FOR OVER 30 YEARS."

TOO BAD I CAN'T SEND YOU.

I DIDN'T SEE ANY AGE LIMIT.

WHO'S THE OLD SHARK DUDE? A CAMP COUNSELOR?

NOPE.

CAMP WINWAH

HIS NAME'S SHERMAN. HE'S ONE OF THE CAMPERS.

WEIRD.

MUNCH MUNCH MUNCH

GO TALK TO HIM. HE'S COOL.

I NEVER KNOW WHAT TO SAY TO OLD FOLKS.

CAMP WINWAH

WHAT WERE THE DINOSAURS REALLY LIKE?

RUNTS LIKE YOU GET STUCK IN MY DENTURES.

SHERMAN'S LAGOON

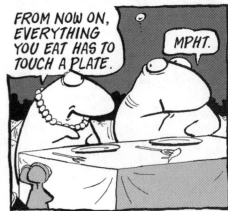

LOOKS LIKE THE LAGOON TRIBUNE GOT SOME ADVERTISERS AGAIN.

"DO YOU SUFFER FROM EMBARRASSING SHELL ODOR?"

GLAD *I* DON'T SUFFER FROM THAT.

OF COURSE YOU DON'T...

IT'S THE REST OF US WHO SUFFER.

HIGH FIVE.

THE NEWSPAPER'S NEW ADVERTISERS ARE EMBARRASSING AND OFFENSIVE!

OH, PLEASE. YOU'RE OVER-REACTING AS USUAL.

I RUN THE SAME FAMILY-ORIENTED NEWSPAPER I'VE ALWAYS RUN.

"WILLY'S CHOWDER BAR. TRY OUR TOPLESS OYSTERS."

OKAY. THAT ONE WOULD BE MORE DAD-ORIENTED.

OKAY, I RELENTED. I PULLED ALL THE OFFENSIVE ADVERTISING FROM MY NEWSPAPER.

AS A MATTER OF FACT, I PULLED **ALL** THE ADS. THE LAGOON TRIBUNE IS NOW A COMMERCIAL-FREE, NON-PARTISAN, OBJECTIVE COMMUNITY WATCHDOG. READ.

"IN HIS ADDRESS TO THE CITY COUNCIL LAST NIGHT, THE MAYOR VOICED HIS CONCERNS ABOUT THE SCHOOL BUDGET..."

"... AS HE SIPPED HIS COOL, REFRESHING DIET 7-UP."

PRODUCT PLACEMENTS NOT WITHSTANDING.

SHERMAN'S LAGOON

GREAT DINNER PARTY, MEGAN.

THANKS, FILLMORE.

AND THINGS ARE JUST GETTING STARTED.

AFTER DESSERT, I THOUGHT WE COULD PLAY SOME BOARD GAMES.

DESSERT! OH MY GOSH! YOU WANTED ME TO BRING A DESSERT!!

I COMPLETELY FORGOT.

NOT A PROBLEM.

A GOOD HOSTESS KNOWS HOW TO IMPROVISE.

SINCE WHEN IS ROLLING IN SUGAR PART OF SCRABBLE?

HOUSE RULES.

SHERMAN'S LAGOON

SHERMAN'S LAGOON

OKAY, SHERMAN, WE'VE GOT FIRST SHIFT OF THE PELICAN WATCH.

AND REMEMBER... THIS IS WAR! IT'S DIRTY, NASTY, AND MEAN OUT THERE!

GRRR.

HOME-MADE LEMON SQUARE?

OOH, LOVELY.

WE'VE ELIMINATED YOUR PELICAN PROBLEM.

IT'S SAFE TO SWIM AROUND NOW.

WHAT DID YOU DO TO HIM?

WE LURED HIM OVER TO ANOTHER LAGOON WHERE HE WON'T BE BOTHERING YOU.

OUR BILL.

SO, YOU DIDN'T REALLY ELIMINATE OUR PROBLEM, YOU JUST MADE IT SOMEBODY ELSE'S.

OTHERWISE WE'D BE OUT OF WORK.

TAP TAP TAP

WHAT'S THIS?

THE STOCK MARKET CLEANED ME OUT. I NEED CASH.

THAT BAD, HUH?

AFRAID SO. I'M BROKE.

RED LOBSTER'S HIRING.

BUSBOYS?

APPETIZERS.

SHERMAN'S LAGOON

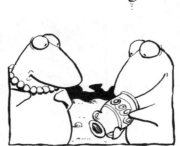

EBAY, HERE WE COME.

WAS THAT WHAT I THINK IT WAS?

YEP. AN ORIGINAL PICASSO. ONLY $30.

YARD SALE

I SAW IT FIRST, BUT I PASSED.

HOW COULD YOU SEE A PICASSO FOR 30 BUCKS AND NOT BUY IT?

I DIDN'T CARE FOR THE FRAME.

AUGH!

I'M ASKING 5 BUCKS FOR THE CLOCK.

BUT, IT'S BROKEN.

YARD SALE

NO IT'S NOT. IT'S JUST PERMANENTLY SET TO 2:34. THAT MEANS, TWICE A DAY IT'S EXACTLY RIGHT.

AS OPPOSED TO FILLMORE'S FANCY SCHMANCY WATCH, WHICH IS ALWAYS 5 MINUTES FAST...

TWICE-A-DAY RIGHT, NEVER RIGHT. WHICH WOULD YOU RATHER OWN?

I'LL TAKE IT.

IS THIS ANOTHER ONE OF HAWTHORNE'S ORNATE, GAWDY THINGS THAT YOU BOUGHT AT HIS YARD SALE?

YEAH. CHECK IT OUT. THE METICULOUS HAND STITCHING...

THE BEAUTIFUL GOLD INLAY. THE GRECO-ROMAN MYTHOLOGY THEME.

THAT'S QUITE A THROW PILLOW.

IT'S A WHOOPIE CUSHION.

SHERMAN'S LAGOON

SHERMAN'S LAGOON

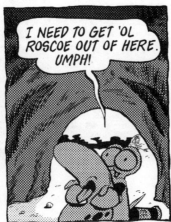

SHERMAN'S LAGOON

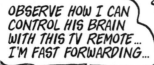

SHERMAN'S LAGOON

SHERMAN'S LAGOON

Best Was
YANORE D
1-800-624-2888
3458   WAAA DANA